SPOTLIGHT ON NATIONS

GERMANY

JOE TISCHLER

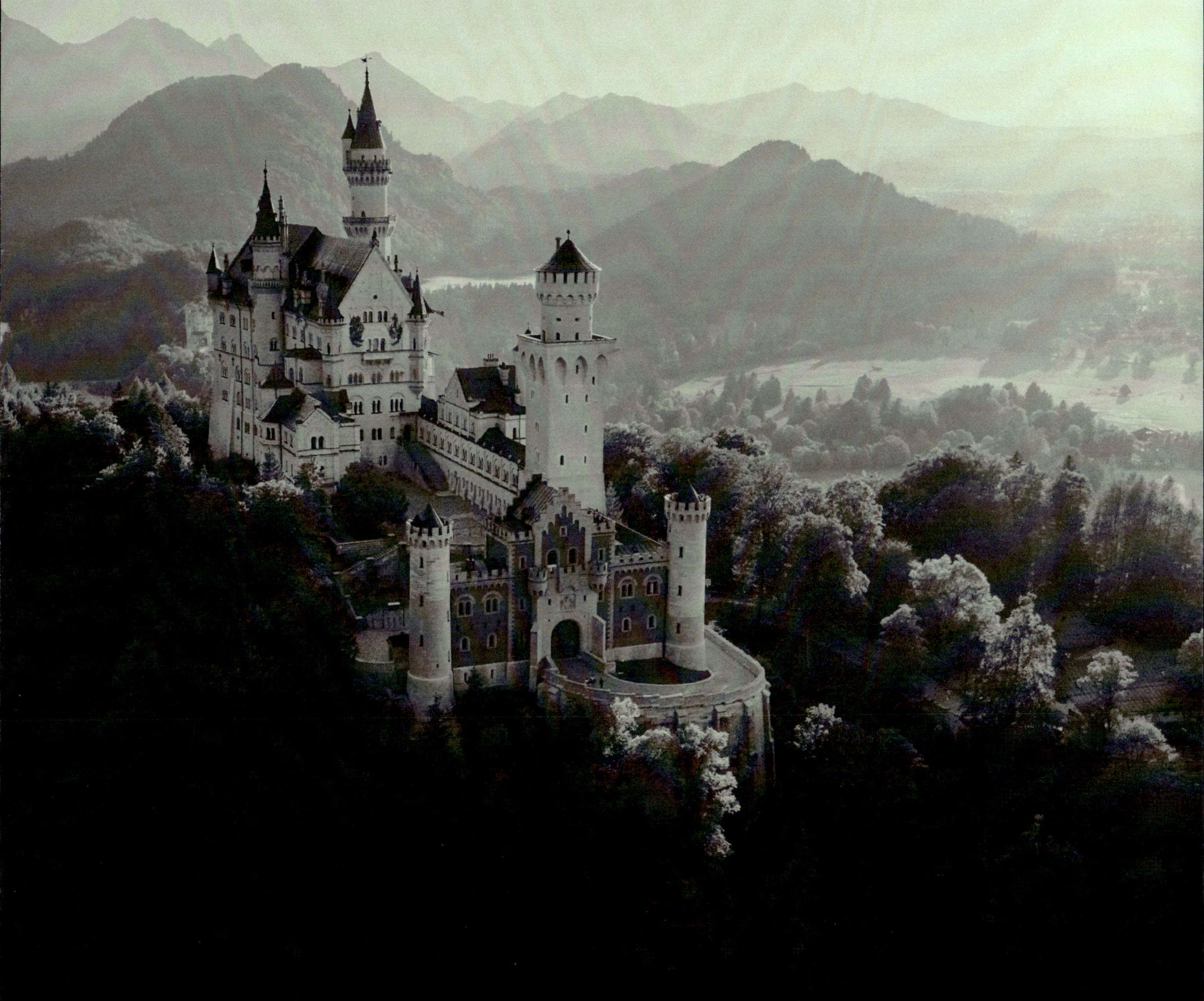

CREATIVE EDUCATION · CREATIVE PAPERBACKS

Published by Creative Education and Creative Paperbacks
P.O. Box 227, Mankato, Minnesota 56002
Creative Education and Creative Paperbacks are imprints
of The Creative Company
www.thecreativecompany.us

Design and production by Blue Design, Inc.
Art direction by Graham Morgan
Edited by Ana Brauer

Photographs by Getty Images/Colin Campbell, 17, Cyril Gosselin, 10, Historical, 14, instamatics, 24, Manuel Romano/NurPhoto, 27; Pexels/Johannes Rampp, 16; Shutterstock/Karl Allgaeuer, 21; Unsplash/Julia Solonina, 3, 28, Martin Katler, cover, 1, Ricardo Gomez Angel, 4–5; Wikimedia Commons/ Albrecht Dürer, 6, Ansgar Koreng / CC BY-SA 3.0 (DE), 12, El Grafo, 29, Granada, 26, Joseph Karl Stieler, 23, Markburger83, 18, Monster4711, 15, public domain, 8, 9, 10, 14, 16, 20, 22, SDASM Archives, 11

Library of Congress Cataloging-in-Publication Data
Names: Tischler, Joe author
Title: Germany / Joe Tischler.
Description: Mankato, Minnesota : Creative Education and Creative Paperbacks, [2026] | Series: Spotlight on nations | Includes bibliographical references and index. | Audience: Ages 10-13 | Audience: Grades 4-6 | Summary: "Explore Germany's history, geography, government, economy, and cultural heritage, plus its global influence and resilience. Written for middle-grade readers, this book includes timelines, sidebars, glossary, resources, and index"-- Provided by publisher.
Identifiers: LCCN 2025018210 (print) | LCCN 2025018211 (ebook) | ISBN 9798895810712 library binding | ISBN 9798896800248 paperback | ISBN 9798895811979 ebook
Subjects: LCSH: Germany--History--Juvenile literature | Germany--Politics and government--Juvenile literature | Germany--Geography--Juvenile literature | LCGFT: Literature
Classification: LCC DD89 .T57 2026 (print) | LCC DD89 (ebook) | DDC 943--dc23/eng/20250715
LC record available at https://lccn.loc.gov/2025018210
LC ebook record available at https://lccn.loc.gov/2025018211

Printed in the United States

CONTENTS

DARK TIMES AND HOPE

Germany is a country filled with history, traditions, and fascinating stories. The country is located in the center of Europe. The Baltic Sea and the North Sea border it to the north. The Alps Mountain Range borders it to the south. Germany has been a major influence on the world for centuries.

Long ago, Germany was made up of small kingdoms and towns, each with its own unique culture. In 1871, these kingdoms united into a single, strong nation. However, Germany's history has not always been easy. The country faced dark times during the world wars, and the country was again divided for decades. Yet, the fall of the Berlin Wall in 1989 marked a new beginning, showing Germany's strength and hope for the future.

Today, Germany is famous for many things. It is the home of Oktoberfest, tasty foods like bratwurst and pretzels, and fairy tales such as *Hansel and Gretel*. Germany is also known for its cars, music, and technology. Whether you visit the peaceful countryside or busy cities like Berlin and Munich, there is always something amazing to discover.

A True Empire

By the time of his death in 814, Charlemagne ruled most of Western Europe, including present-day France, Germany, Belgium, the Netherlands, and parts of Italy.

CHAPTER ONE

HISTORY

The history of Germany can be traced back more than 2,000 years. Long ago, the Romans ruled over an area called Germania. Different tribes, including the Celts, Vandals, Goths, and Saxons, fought to gain control of the land. By the 8th century, these tribes were united by a leader named Charlemagne. He was crowned Holy Roman Emperor by Pope Leo III (3) in the year 800. The Holy Roman Empire included what is now Germany, France, the Netherlands, and northern Italy.

After Charlemagne died in 814, princes and dukes became powerful. They became rulers of their own territories. They created their own laws and controlled their own armies. The Roman Catholic Church was beginning to gain power in Germany.

In the 16th century, a monk named Martin Luther ignited the Protestant Reformation. He had a list of 95 complaints against the Roman Catholic Church. This religious divide led to decades of conflict. This included the Thirty Years' War (1618–48). It devastated Germany. Its population and

MILESTONES IN GERMAN HISTORY

800

▸ Charlemagne is crowned emperor of the Holy Roman Empire

1517

▸ Martin Luther sparks the Protestant Reformation by posting his 95 Theses

agriculture were decimated due to the fighting on the land. The Peace of Westphalia was signed in 1648, putting an end to the war.

After the Holy Roman Empire ended in the early 1800s, Germany was made up of many **city-states**. One leader, Otto von Bismarck, helped bring them together. By 1871, he created the German Empire after winning wars against Denmark, Austria, and France. Germany became powerful, especially in industry and military affairs. Tensions began to grow in Europe, and World War I (1914–18) began. German forces invaded nearby countries but later surrendered. The Treaty of Versailles punished Germany, leading to many years of economic and political instability.

In 1933, Adolf Hitler and the Nazi Party came to power in Germany. Hitler blamed Jewish people for many of Germany's problems. Millions

Cologne

Giovanni Maria Farina invented cologne in Cologne, Germany, in 1709. His refreshing citrus fragrance became famous worldwide. The city remains associated with this scent.

—— HISTORICAL HIGHLIGHT ——

The Iron Chancellor

Otto von Bismarck was known as the "Iron Chancellor" because of his strong and determined leadership. Bismarck believed in using diplomacy and sometimes war to achieve his goals. He was the first Chancellor of the German Empire in 1871. He led Germany through wars against Denmark, Austria, and France that helped unite the German states. Bismarck introduced social reforms, like health insurance and pensions, to help workers. He wanted to make Germany strong and stable, but he also worked to keep peace in Europe by forming alliances with other countries.

of Jewish people were killed in the Holocaust. In 1939, Germany invaded Poland, starting World War II. In 1945, sensing defeat, Hitler committed suicide, and Germany surrendered. The war left Germany in ruins. The country was split into two countries. West Germany was **democratic** while East Germany became **communist**. The city of Berlin was also divided. In 1961, a tall wall was built to separate East and West Berlin.

Protesters brought down the Berlin Wall in 1989, and by 1990, Germany became one nation again. Germany has since become a stable democracy, an economic powerhouse, and a key player in the **European Union**.

1618–48

> The Thirty Years' War devastates Germany

1871

> Germany is unified under Otto von Bismarck, who becomes the first German chancellor

Christmas

The tradition of decorating Christmas trees started in Germany in the 16th century. Martin Luther is often credited with adding candles to trees, inspired by starlight through the forest.

HISTORICAL  HIGHLIGHT

The Printing Press

Johannes Gutenberg was a German inventor. He changed the world with his creation of the printing press around 1440. Before his invention, books were copied by hand, which was slow and expensive. Gutenberg's printing press made it possible to produce books much faster and at a lower cost. The key to the printing press's success was Gutenberg's development of movable type. These were small, reusable metal blocks with letters on them. Printers could arrange the blocks to form words and pages, then press them onto paper using ink. His invention helped spread ideas and education, leading to important movements like the Reformation.

German pilots in
WORLD WAR I
were
highly skilled.

1914–18
1919
Germany plays a central role in World War I
The Treaty of Versailles imposes harsh penalties on Germany

Government Building

The Reichstag Building is where Germany's government meets. It was built in Berlin in 1894. A fire damaged it in 1933, and it stayed empty for many years. After Germany reunited in 1990, the building was fixed. Today, it has a glass dome that visitors can walk through!

GOVERNMENT

Unified Germany has a democratic system of government. This means people vote to choose their leaders. Germany is a federal **parliamentary** republic. Power is shared between different levels of government. The head of the government is the chancellor. They are elected to a term of four years, with no limit to how many terms a chancellor can serve. The chancellor leads the country and makes important decisions. The chancellor is chosen by the Bundestag.

The Bundestag is one of two parts of Germany's parliament. It directly represents the people of Germany, and its members are elected in national elections. It is responsible for debating and passing laws. The other part of parliament is called the Bundesrat. It represents the country's 16 states. It ensures the states have input in making laws, especially those that affect all of Germany.

In addition to having a chancellor, Germany also has a president. The president of Germany does not have much of a role in the government. Their role is more ceremonial. The president represents Germany in diplomatic events and performs duties like appointing officials.

1933

▸ Adolf Hitler becomes Chancellor, leading to the Nazi era

1945

▸ Germany is a major force in World War II

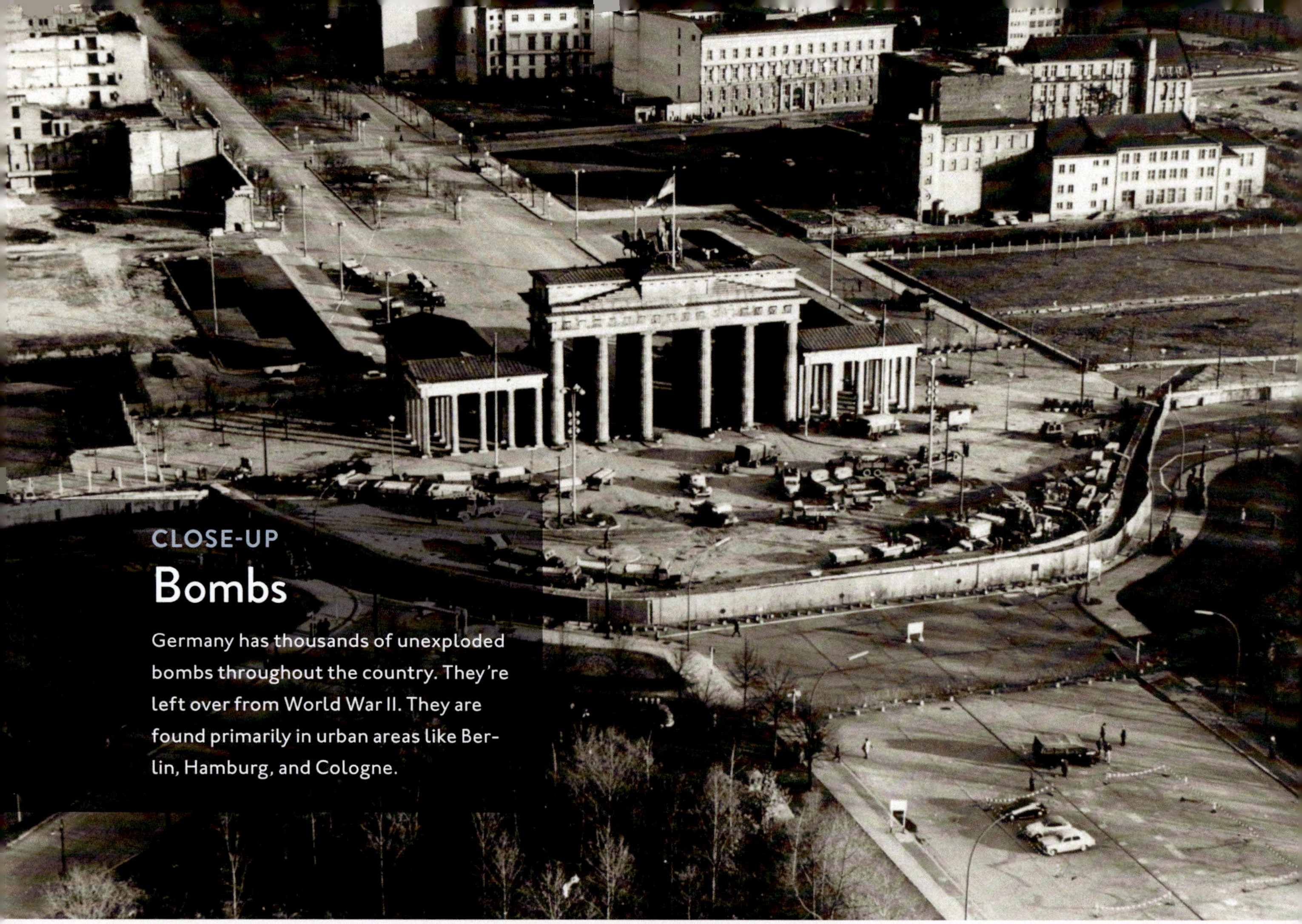

HISTORICAL HIGHLIGHT

The Berlin Wall

The Berlin Wall stood in the middle of Berlin from 1961 to 1989. After World War II, Germany was split into an East (controlled by the Soviet Union) and a West (supported by the United States and its allies) Germany. The wall was built by East Germany to stop people from escaping to the West, where life was more prosperous. The wall was made of concrete and barbed wire, with guards and watchtowers. People risked their lives trying to cross it. In 1989, changes in politics and protests led to the fall of the wall. East Germany's government announced that people could cross freely, and citizens began tearing down the wall. Today, parts of the wall remain as a reminder of the past.

Germany has a federal system of government. This means that power is shared between the national government and the government of its states. Each state has its own authority over areas like education and police. The national government handles bigger issues like defense and foreign relations.

Germany has one of the largest and strongest economies in the world. It is a social market economy. This concept combines free-market principles with social policies to promote fairness and protect citizens.

The country is a global leader in manufacturing, particularly in industries like automobiles, machinery, and chemicals. Exports play a big role in Germany's economy. The country exports a wide range of products all over the world, from cars to high-tech machines. Small and medium-sized businesses help drive innovation, create jobs, and keep the economy diverse and competitive.

The euro is Germany's **currency**. It has been the country's official currency since 2002. Its previous currency was the Deutsche mark. The euro is used by 20 of the 27 European Union countries. It is managed by the European Central Bank and provides convenience for trade and travel across member nations.

1949	1961
▸ West Germany and East Germany are officially established	▸ The Berlin Wall is built, dividing East and West Berlin

Location

Many castles were built on mountain-tops or near trade routes for defense and control.

HISTORICAL  **HIGHLIGHT**

Castles of Germany

Germany is famous for its castles. When you walk inside one, it feels like you are stepping into a fairy tale. There are more than 20,000 castles across the country. Many were built hundreds of years ago as homes for kings, knights, and nobles. These castles also served as fortresses, protecting the people inside from enemies during wars. One of the most famous castles is Neuschwanstein Castle. It is located near the border of Germany and Austria. It was the inspiration for Disney's Sleeping Beauty castle. Today, many castles are open to visitors where people can learn about their history and imagine what life was like in the past.

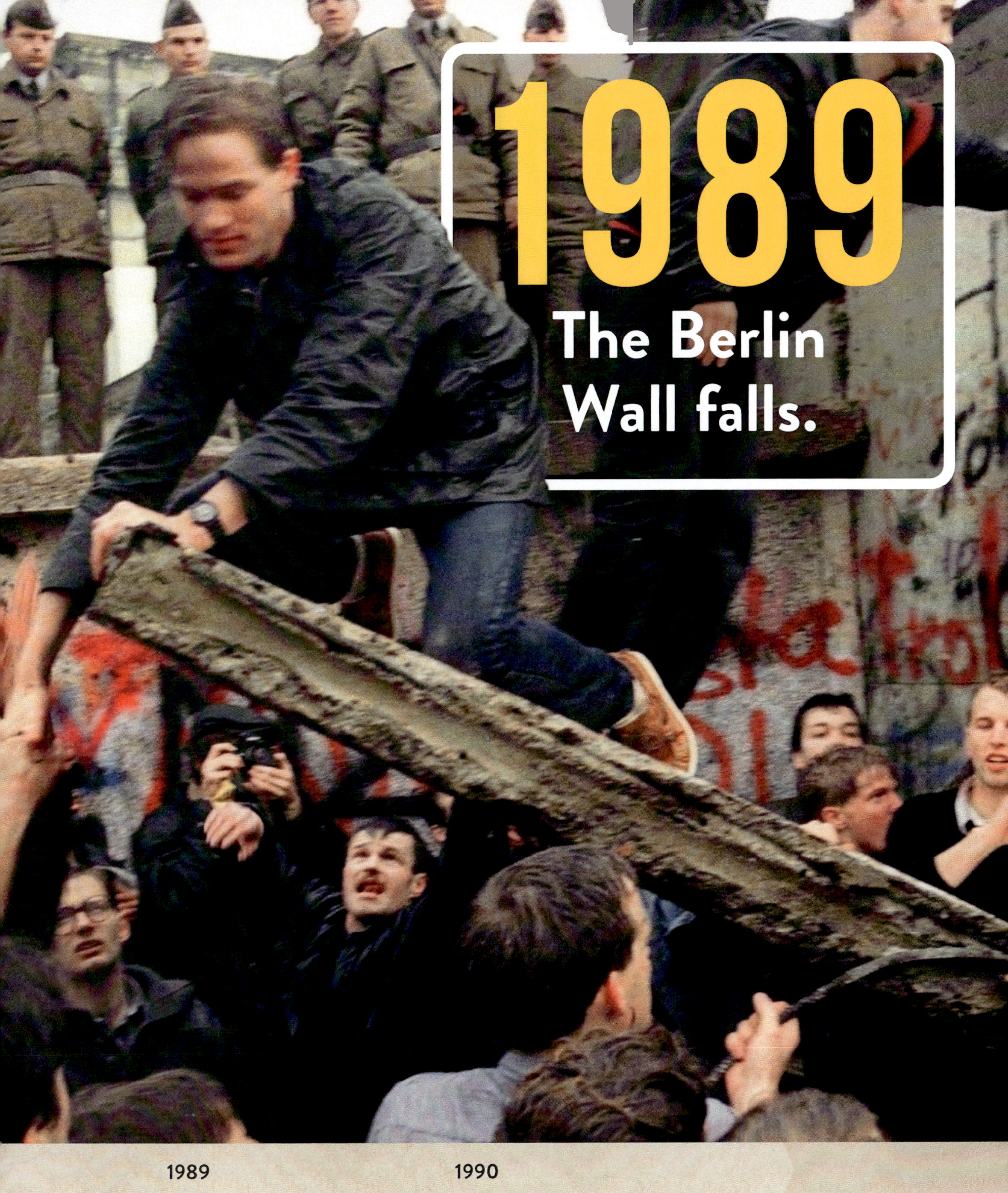

1989
The Berlin Wall falls.

1989
1990
The Berlin Wall falls
Germany is reunified as one nation

CLOSE-UP
Beer

Germany has more than 1,500 types of
beer. The country has beer purity laws
that date back to 1516. These laws say
that beer can only be made using three
ingredients: water, barley, and hops.

Festzelt

Himmel der Bayern

CHAPTER THREE

PEOPLE, CULTURE, AND TRADITIONS

Germany is a country rich in history shaped by centuries of art, music, philosophy, and traditions. Germany has a population of about 83 million people. It is one of the most populous countries in Europe. The official language is German. Most Germans are fluent in the language. Regional dialects and accents give each area its own flavor.

Germany is known for its diversity. **Immigration** has played a key role in shaping the country. People from Turkey, Poland, Italy, and other nations have become part of the German society. They've brought their own traditions, food, and culture. This has added to Germany's cultural landscape.

German culture is rooted in its history and contributions to the arts and sciences. Albert Einstein was born in Germany. He is one of the greatest scientists of all time. Other famous German figures include writer Johann Wolfgang von Goethe and philosopher Immanuel Kant. These three highlight Germany's influence on the world. Germans value education, creativity, and intellectual pursuits.

2002

Germany adopts the euro as its currency

Music is a big part of German culture. Germany has given the world legendary composers like Ludwig van Beethoven, Johann Sebastian Bach, and Richard Wagner. From classical orchestras to modern electronic music scenes, Germans celebrate a wide variety of sounds.

Germans take pride in their beer, especially during events like Oktoberfest. German food is hearty and includes dishes like bratwurst, sauerkraut, pretzels, and schnitzel. Germans love their desserts, too, like the black forest cake.

Germans celebrate many unique traditions and festivals that reflect their history and values. They observe Christmas with great enthusiasm. Nearly every German town sets up a market for Christmas. These feature wooden stalls filled with handmade crafts, ornaments, food, and wine. The markets are a cornerstone of German Christmas traditions. They create a cozy and festive atmosphere.

—— HISTORICAL HIGHLIGHT ——

Oktoberfest

Oktoberfest is one of Germany's most famous celebrations held every year in Munich. It began in 1810 as a royal wedding celebration but grew into a big festival over time. Oktoberfest starts in late September and lasts about two weeks, welcoming millions of visitors from around the world. People gather in large tents to enjoy traditional German food like pretzels, sausages, and roast chicken. They also drink specially brewed Oktoberfest beer, served in huge mugs. Music, dancing, and colorful parades make the event more exciting.

2005

▸ Angela Merkel becomes Germany's first female chancellor

Another important tradition is Karneval or Fasching. It is a carnival season celebrated in February. It blends joy, tradition, and cultural expression. People dress up in colorful costumes, attend parades, and enjoy festivities that bring together communities.

Germany's 16 states each have their own unique traditions. Bavaria is known for its alpine festivals and distinctive dress. In northern Germany, traditions like herring festivals often revolve around the sea.

Germany also respects cultural traditions like environmental consciousness. Germans are known for being organized and valuing time, as well as for their efforts to preserve the environment. Recycling is a big part of everyday life. The country invests heavily in renewable energy and sustainability.

Cuckoo

The cuckoo clock was first created in the Black Forest region of Germany. It is famous for its detailed carvings and chirping cuckoo bird. These clocks are a popular souvenir for visitors.

HISTORICAL  **HIGHLIGHT**

The Brothers Grimm

Brothers Jacob and Wilhelm Grimm were German storytellers who lived from late-18th century to mid-19th century. They gave the world some of the best-known folktales of all time. Their work, *Grimm's Fairy Tales*, includes iconic stories such as *Cinderella*, *Snow White*, *Hansel and Gretel*, and *Rapunzel*. Their stories have shaped film, theater, and music with adaptations. Walt Disney drew inspiration from Grimms' tales to produce beloved animations like *Snow White and the Seven Dwarfs*. Additionally, the Grimms contributed to language, developing the concept of "Grimm's Law," which explains phonetic changes in languages.

LUDWIG VAN BEETHOVEN

2018
Germany achieves record renewable energy production

2020
Germany leads effort to combat Covid-19 in Europe

CHAPTER FOUR

GERMANY TODAY

Germany is the seventh largest country in Europe. But it's still smaller than some U.S. states, like Texas and Alaska. The country has a **temperate** climate. Its weather is shaped by its location in central Europe and by the nearby seas to the north.

Each of Germany's states has its own **coat of arms.** Bavaria is the largest state. It is located in the southern part of the country. Munich is the largest city in Bavaria. BMW, Audi, Puma, and Adidas all have factories in Munich. The state of North Rhine-Westphalia has the most people. Cars, light aircraft, and machinery are all made there.

Germany is a global and political power. It has the largest economy in Europe. German companies, especially in fields like automotive, engineering, and renewable energy, are major players on the international stage. Germany is a leading voice in the European Union. It plays a critical role in shaping European Union policies. It is also a member of important international organizations such as the United Nations (UN), Group of Seven (G7), and Group of Twenty (G20).

Soccer is the most popular sport in Germany. The top professional soccer league is the Bundesliga. Bayern Munich and Borussia Dortmund

World Cup Stars

are two of its best teams. The German men's national team performs well on the world stage. They have won four FIFA World Cups. The last one came in 2014.

Germany is one of the leading motorsports countries in the world. German companies BMW and Mercedes-Benz are lead manufacturers in motorsports. Another German company, Porsche, has won the 24 Hours of Le Mans racing event 19 times. German driver Michael Schumacher set many records in his career. He won seven Formula One (F1) World Drivers' Championships. He is tied with Lewis Hamilton for the most titles in F1 history.

Germany plays an important role in the fashion industry. Berlin is one of the fashion capitals of the world. It is home to Berlin Fashion Week. Young and creative German fashion designers show off their creations at this event. A well-known opera festival called the Bayreuth Festival is held every summer. It is dedicated to the works of Richard Wagner. The Berlin International Film Festival is held every February. It is one of the world's most prestigious film festivals.

Germany has a rich and vast history. It faced devastation from its involvement in World War I and II. It has built itself up to a leading global power. It is a testament to its ability to adapt, innovate, and collaborate.

GERMANY

Continent: Europe

Capital: Berlin

Population: 83.28 million

National language: German

Government: Federal parliamentary republic

Currency: Euro

Main Religion: Christianity

Flag Colors: Black, red, gold

National Flower: Cornflower

WORDS to Know

city-state a historical city with its own rulers and laws that were valid inside the city walls

coat of arms a unique symbol or design representing a family, individual, or organization

communist a type of government and economic system in which goods are owned in common and available to all as needed

currency standardized money in any form

democratic political system where everyone is equal and has the right to vote

European Union political and economic union of 27 European countries

immigration process of moving to a different country to live for an extended period of time

parliament law-making body of a country

temperate neither hot nor cold with balanced seasonal weather patterns

LEARN MORE

Books

Dickmann, Nancy. *Your Passport to Germany*. North Mankato, Minn.: Capstone Press, 2023.

Sorenson, Matthew. *Exploring Germany!: And its Special Places, History, and Culture*. Independently published, 2025.

Walker, Tracy Sue. *Spotlight on Germany*. Minneapolis: Lerner Publications, 2024.

Websites

"Germany." Britannica Kids.

https://kids.britannica.com/kids/article/Germany/345694

"Germany." National Geographic Kids. https://kids.nationalgeographic.com/geography/countries/article/germany

"Germany Travel Guide." Kids World Travel Guide.

https://www.kids-world-travel-guide.com/germany-travel-guide.html

Documentaries

History of Germany. Fire of Learning, 2018. https://www.youtube.com/watch?v=0ZR9B2KIJBI&t=8s

How Was Germany Formed? Knowledgia, 2024, https://www.youtube.com/watch?v=fjPJQeClSIY

History of Germany. Balkan Odyssey, 2021. https://www.youtube.com/watch?v=5i9PpE8yu2s

Visit

BRANDENBURG GATE

Visit one of Germany's most iconic land-marks that symbolizes unity and peace. It stood near the Berlin Wall. The Gate turned into a symbol of reunification and hope for a united Germany.
Pariser Platz, 10117 Berlin, Germany

OLYMPIC STADIUM

Visit the place where the 1936 Summer Olympics were held, where U.S. sprinter Jesse Owens won four gold medals. A street outside the stadium is named after him.
Olympischer Platz 3, 14053 Berlin, Germany

NEUSCHWANSTEIN CASTLE

Visit the castle that inspired Disney's Sleeping Beauty castle. It offers breath-taking views of the Bavarian Alps.
Neuschwansteinstrasse 20, 87645 Schwangau, Bavaria, Germany

WARTBURG CASTLE

Visit one of the castles known for its connection to Martin Luther. He trans-lated the New Testament here.
Auf der Wartburg 1, 99817 Eisenach, Thuringia, Germany

INDEX